What Is Not a Miracle

◦◎◦

Don Badgley

A Publication of The Poetry Box®

Poems ©2021 Don Badgley
All rights reserved.

Editing & Book Design by Shawn Aveningo Sanders
Cover Design by Shawn Aveningo Sanders
Cover Photo by Robert R. Sanders (RobertSandersPhoto.com)
Author Photo by Michael Gold

No part of this book may be reproduced in any manner whatsoever without permission from the author, except in the case of brief quotations embodied in critical essays, reviews and articles.

ISBN: 978-1-948461-87-0
Printed in the United States of America.
Wholesale Distribution via Ingram.

Published by The Poetry Box®, 2021
Portland, Oregon
ThePoetryBox.com

Dedicated to Dad;
George Albert Badgley
(1909 -2008)

He gave me poetry and pointed toward the Light
as he let his life speak.

The principal theme of this collection is centered on the spiritual realm or on the natural world and for me, these are often indistinguishable. The poems are deeply influenced by my life as a Friend, "Quaker." I offer them as a glimpse of one man's corporeal and spiritual journey.

It is my hope that these small poetic offerings may kindle recognition of the Light within each of us and so affirm the infinite, eternal and unchangeable Ground of Being that is our universal Source. Or perhaps they may simply serve to trigger a smile of recognition.

Contents

I.
My Tree	9
Beginnings	10
Grass Temple	11
Early Riser	12

II.
What Is Not a Miracle	15
Eternity	16
Dragonfly	17
There Are Days	18
Moments	19
February Oaks	20
Light Rain	21
Easter	22
April Acting March	23
Owl	24

III.
Airport Evangelical	27
Soldiers' Cry	28
He Asked Me to Explain	29
Remnant	30
Spring in the Rose Garden	31
Weep for the Executioner	32
Rage	33

IV.

Fleeting	37
Tetawabca	38
The Spark	39
The Sun Though Low	40
Silver Bay	41
September	42
Look Now to the Hills	43
My Fears	44
Becoming	45
Morning Hope	46

V.

Meeting for Worship	49
The Stranger	50
In Silence	51
The Mountain of Peace	52

VI.

Easy Memories	55
Reach	56

About the Author	59
About The Poetry Box®	60

~I~

My sense of the Divine was part of my awareness from an early age. I could not have named it. That perception of the ineffable Spirit continues to evolve.

I begin as it began....

My Tree

There was a maple in my yard
That as a boy I climbed for solitude
Amid the crimson leaves
And golden light of autumn afternoons
A secret, timeless place
Where Grace became Peace
The Eternal smelled of life
And was full within me.

Beginnings

During that summer
Not long after the universe
Came into being,
For me
Dirt roads were the way
And pavement began some miles away.
Those dusty roads were safe
For the old American bike
That carried me
From farm to farm
Smokey the dog scouting ahead
With earth scents and manure
And hay and fertilizer
And corn and apples
And I knew peace.

Grass Temple

Back when summer grass
Was a temple I lay upon
To touch the face of god
And feel my Source beneath
There came a moment…
Just a moment
Of lighted clarity
And I seek it still
With awareness
And blissful certainty.

Early Riser

I get up before the rest
To find the corner in the dining room
Where first sun warms the floor.

This is my special spot
A place of brief solitude,
Blissful and centered in the light.

The family still rests upstairs
And then, my father passes by
On his way to the kitchen.

He smiles, and quietly says "warm,"
And that voice and all it means
Comforts me still.

~II~

The title poem for this collection connects the spiritual and mystical with the natural world which always seems to point directly toward the Source. I was taught that a "miracle" is unexplainable, a logically impossible and supernatural event. Each day that I pass through the continuum that is life, it becomes clearer that the very existence of my conscious self, life and awareness seems to fit that definition precisely. Miracles abound. I no longer search for them. They simply are. I live my days noticing them.

What Is Not a Miracle

What is not a miracle?
Must I look to the stars or holy books,
Or measure my poor understanding
By the infinite unknown?
Must I witness the healing of the lame or blind,
Or the raising of the dead?
Is the air I breathe not wonder enough,
And is my own clear sight an insufficient gift
To perceive the falling leaf,
Or sunlight captured by the dew?
Should I discount the scent of rain in spring,
Or the music of spoken love,
Or the fullness of the universe,
Just beneath the petal of a rose?

Eternity

The miracle of life defies the mind,
Or poor attempts to quantify our place
Within the infinite, yet still we find,
That love has countered dread and offered grace,
A peace that balances our fear of death,
As we become aware that age or youth,
Is but an interlude, a single breath,
To the Creator of the living Truth.
We are encircled by the evidence,
The blossoming of spring and waters sweet,
The butterfly emerging from cocoon,
A universe that speaks with eloquence,
If we but still our minds, and thus attune
Our hearts, to that eternal Light we meet.

Dragonfly

A dragonfly appeared as I was being still
And lighted on my shoe to prophesy
She was older than the dinosaurs and still
Connected to the timeless Source.
She didn't speak but cocked a hundred eyes
At *me!*
And encouraged me
To laugh.

There Are Days

There are sometimes days of such striking beauty
That I am stunned into stillness,
Amidst the green cathedral walls
Beneath a vault of purest blue,
Where the cardinal sings his homily
And I the humble congregant
Am grateful just to breathe and worship there.

Moments

We, each of us, have moments
That may remove our restless doubt
And dissolve uncertainty,
Moments that clarify the infinite
And lift us from the muck of ambiguity
Into the well-lit unity of One.
But these, though sought, are few
And if noticed may be dismissed as illusion
As we grimly cling to the darker deceptions
That our earthly flesh requires.

February Oaks

Neither wind nor ice has yet dislodged the curled oaken leaves,
Still clinging to the twigs that soon will green anew
And only then will these brown memories drift down
To kiss and feed the earth again.

Light Rain

This afternoon's light rain, almost a mist
Might bring sadness except that the dogwood
Splashed against the new green rivals the absent sun
And the finches chatter in celebration.

Easter

As Inward Light transforms the tomb of fear,
The stone that is my doubt is rolled away,
And love is risen in my heart.

April Acting March

The sun would not assert itself
To challenge April acting March
Seeming lazy, hidden there
Behind the infinite gray wet
That clings to sky and earth
And to my bones and gooseflesh
Still waiting patiently for Spring.

Owl

Somewhere in the dark
Beyond my open summer window
An owl proclaimed her victory,
Or perhaps a celebration
Of the night near done,
Her crop just filled —
High above the now empty den
Of one that will never see again
The coming dawn.

~III~

If only we could ever reside in these blissful and grace filled moments that are given us by the touch of nature in its infinite majesty. Sadly, the human world intrudes and challenges us to remember our Source and strength and to trust to that Light to comfort and guide us. In these verses that follow the interface of my Quaker path and more worldly concerns finds its voice.

Airport Evangelical

Two men whose accents
Placed their births
Beyond my shores
Were struggling to understand
Their assailant's passion.
One tried in vain to say
That good is good,
That love is love,
But she discounted that,
And beat them mercilessly,
With her certainty,
And brochure scripture
That threatened Hell
And counseled fear,
All in the name of He,
The one who died to prove
His grace and love,
And I smiled for them all,
Keeping still.

Soldiers' Cry

Dear sweet war,
Mocking the sanctity of life,
Proclaimed by ministers of love,
Hypocrites, praying for victory,
Proud practitioners of faith,
Counseling love for our enemies
Killed ten thousand times in every heart,
And corpses pile like withered fruit,
Beneath the dying vines of lost legacy;
A bloodless red witness to the cold,
In that January garden of our souls.

He Asked Me to Explain

He asked me to explain
With a note of confident derision
He asked me to explain
How I, and we, could be so naïve
As to reject the machines of war
That make our nation safe and great
He asked me to explain
What I would do when the other came
To destroy our holy constitution
And slaughter my family and his
He asked me to explain…

And I could not explain
The Experience of sacred Light
That re-orders us to offer love
Even to our enemies
I could only point toward the Source
The Source that can only explain itself.

Remnant

Never has there been a time,
When generals, politicians, citizens and priests,
Have not proclaimed their love of peace,
The peace that is the heart of their religion's cause,
Whether Muslim, Jew or follower of Christ,
They all unite for peace with pious certainty,
Despite the truth of lust made manifest,
In every celebration of the fruits of war;
The glorious heroes, the flags, the blood and sacrifice,
The righteous cause, the martyrs and the patriots,
Each conspire to justify the "sacred" ends,
While corpses litter time and history,
In silent witness to the universal love of peace.

Yet still, a hidden remnant gathers silently,
In the presence of a Light unchangeable, Divine,
That utterly denies the arms of war,
They walk across the earth with joy,
And offer love unqualified, as Friends
And children of the Light.

Spring in the Rose Garden

Spring comes quietly to an arid land,
Where through the barren ground a single bloom
Pushes forth to light and fragile life,
Trembling crimson in a perfect hope.
A sudden shadow reaches out to her,
And a boot heel crushes this small miracle
Beneath the warrior towering above,
He blossoming and brave at twenty years.
The enemy unseen contains his rage,
His certainty perfects unhurried aim,
And hollow-pointed steel spits out its curse,
Into the flowering face of youthful dreams.
And there, upon his knees, another dies,
As blood and darkened petals merge in dust,
And in a distant land the leader prays
Into the rose and cherry scented air.

Weep for the Executioner

~for Saddam

Weep for the executioner
Weep for the cheering mob
Reaching for death
Weep for the condemned
Now reduced to frailty
And when you have wept yourself dry
And gasp for air
Raise your eyes to heaven,
The source of Love inspired tears
And know that the ocean of Light
Was never touched by darkness
And weep again for joy.

Rage

~for George Floyd and countless others

Tentacles of rage embrace us
Blisters weeping in their grip
Rage, our overseer and his whip
Venomous rage, defiling our skin
Rage, our helpless limbic rejoinder
To filthy injustice
Rage, crushing out our breath
Vomiting from our shredded lips
In righteous gasps
RAGE,
The oppressor's final victory.

~IV~

Then, at the juncture of the secular world and the spirit world there are observations, experiences, wonders and dreams. There are celebrations and simple joys. There is life stretching toward an unknown future and stretching behind with the foundations of what will be. It is a certainty that the brushstrokes of God are painted on human awareness.

Fleeting

How compelling is this whispered call,
This need to change the pace, the course,
And blind inertia of immutable reality,
Though we are but as embers blown aloft,
In a maelstrom eight billion souls across,
Our heat fleeting, drifting toward oblivion,
We remain aware, we see, we feel, we know,
And should our light endure to reach its source,
Falling into the pure tinder of divine love,
It will surely kindle a blaze that burns anew,
Altering the infinite beyond our time.

Tetawabca

The infant at her breast was unaware,
Except of warmth and sustenance
That he accepted as his right as lord,
And she, though but a child herself,
Was resting in the certainty of peace
As ancient as the universe new-born,
Before constraints of space and time
Could separate the light from dark,
And only love was infinite.

The Spark

My walk through life,
Sometimes a run,
Sometimes a crawl
And sometimes slinking backward
Toward the shadows
Has ever been lighted
By a sense of my being more
Than a lump of sentient glop,
And even when cowering
In the shadow of despair
There is that flash of certainty,
Like a single sparkle
On pristine snow
That speaks of something
Bright and constant
That remains untouched
Within me,
Safe, unafraid and essential,
And there I rest, recover and trust
To the Eternal
From which — and to which
I ever rise.

The Sun Though Low

It was one of those autumn days
That forces pause to celebrate,
The sun now low in the southern sky,
Was striking bright, rejoicing
In remaining gold and crimson ornaments.
Then, as if to censure me
(And the eternal King of Light)
A churning wave of clouds and rain
Consumed the world
With the suddenness of a bully's slap,
Conjuring gloom and a dark reminder
Of the deeper chill certain yet to come.

Then the moment passed
And glancing upward from my scribbling
The King had momentarily returned
Just to cover every twig in diamonds.

Silver Bay

Glad shouts sparkled across the lake
Words obscured
But *joy* survived the distance,
Laughter disconnected from the source,
An enchanted resonance
Dancing over rippling waves;
Simple miracles reflecting Love.

September

It still feels like summer but
The shadows have shifted with the tint of trees
And the perennials that line my small world,
Lush and thriving
Seem prepared for rest.

Look Now to the Hills

Look now to the hills
And there to the mountains beyond
Ancient profiles smoothed and rounded
By time beyond human existence
Look there when lamenting your suffering
Look there when filled with self-importance
Lift your eyes to the clouds beyond
And to the sky beyond
And the unseen stars beyond
Look to galaxies
Uncountable and receding forever
And then, sufficiently humbled, look within
And witness the miracle of knowing
Of awareness and of life and of love
And there behold the infinite and essential Truth,
Preceding all else;
And then lift again your eyes to the hills.

My Fears

My fears are as granite colored clouds
Offering the illusion of mountains
Obscuring the true horizon
Where grace resides.

Becoming

At the base of that waterfall
In a faraway land,
Enveloped in its roar and mists
I came to know that
There are no faraway lands,
I was the faraway,
The lost and distant,
As I slow became united
With the Source and immanent eternity
That flowed beside, over, beneath
And within me
And there I awakened,
Becoming the river
Becoming.

Morning Hope

I gaze into the infant day
With boundless trust
That the perfection
Of the dew-covered blossoms
Trembling beside me
Might order the path before me
And I am lifted anew
By the sparrow's song
And nourished by the scent
Of mist filled and sparkling air.

~V~

It is a challenge for Quakers to effectively share with non-members the experience of Friends meeting. The following may be familiar to Friends and I hope offers to others a sense of what it means to be expectantly gathered in the Light. The following four verses give my sense of the Meeting for Worship.

Meeting for Worship

The silence deepens as the morning sun
Lights its passing across the ancient boards,
Placed there by those whose walk through life is done,
So that Friends could gather ever facing towards
The center, where the altar waits unseen,
Devoid of ornaments designed to lead,
Or rituals or rules that come between
The Source Experience and Living Seed.

The meetinghouse is not designed to be
A sacred site but more a place to wait
For strength, to live and carry on the task
Beyond the door, where others long to see
That inward Light is there for all who ask,
Revealed as Love, to share and celebrate.

The Stranger

A stranger came to Meeting first day last,
And crashed into our worshipping, well past
Appointed starting time and stomped his feet,
Then shook his snowy coat and took a seat,

We Friends are quiet folk, considered odd,
In how we think and how we worship God,
And such disturbances are rather rare,
And caused not just a few of us to stare.

His bearded face was rough, his clothes all worn,
His deep-set eyes were dark, his hair unshorn,
Though none of us would think his looks a sin,
Our glances didn't welcome crashing in.

But if he noticed us, it didn't show,
He simply closed his eyes and seemed to grow
All still, and seemed to understand this place,
As gentle calm transformed his weathered face.

The hour passed without a spoken word,
But none would ever say no voice was heard,
And at the meeting's rise we looked upon,
His empty seat to find that he had gone.

In Silence

Gathered
In the place of silence
We Friends embrace simplicity,
Surrendering our hearts to wait,
Together,
Still—within the rising morning light;
Centering to sanctify this space made holy,
Not in form,
But rather by the seed of Love;
Not by altar made of stone,
Or temple's hallowed vault,
But by The Light—Experienced,
Present in our midst,
The infinite—Divine.

The Mountain of Peace

We do not climb the mountain of Peace.
But wait quietly at the bottom,
At the base,
Where living surrounds us
Still crowding our minds.
There we simply pause
Looking upward
Awaiting the stillness,
Awaiting the centering that silences the din,
That covers the artificial light
And reveals a truer Light within.
We wait at the bottom knowing
That we will climb together,
Each lifting the other — though motionless,
Where we *become* the mountain of peace
And discover once again
That the summit was only as far away
As the distance between Compassion and Love.

~VI~

And so, it ends where it began, with memories. Some are deep and hidden, some well-held and constant, these the foundations of who I am and yet will become. The first Advice — "Be still and know…"

Easy Memories

When I reflect upon a sweet return,
To childlike ways and easy memories,
As ash cloaked embers stirred by gentle breeze
Rekindling a youthful hope, I yearn
For rituals and images that burn
Away the seasoned bark that no one sees,
Renewing me within as I appease
The tyrant time, in centered calm sojourn.

And yet, no recollection can restore
The flesh of youth, or ever recreate
The innocence I sought to lose before
I knew or understood that lofty state;
To this, recall is not a weighty chore,
But armor such pure truth will consecrate.

Reach

Dear Friends, let us reach
Reach toward the stillness
Stillness that reveals the Light
Light discovered within
Within the perfect oneness
Oneness with the Eternal
Eternal single moment
Moment,   of endless Grace.

About the Author

Don Badgley is a lifetime resident of the Hudson Valley in New York State. Raised in a rural setting in a Quaker family Don is married and the father of two grown daughters. He remains active with the Religious Society of Friends (Quakers) and is the presiding clerk of his local Quaker meeting in Poughkeepsie, NY. He continues his now 35-year career as an insurance agent.

Don was encouraged to write poetry by his father and has been writing since his youth. This is his first published collection.

About The Poetry Box®

The Poetry Box® is a boutique publishing company in Portland, Oregon, who provides a platform for both established and emerging poets to share their words with the world through beautiful printed books and chapbooks.

Feel free to visit the online bookstore (thePoetryBox.com), where you'll find more titles including:

Matrimony by Laurel Feigenbaum

Nothing More to Lose by Carolyn Martin

Notes from a Caregiver by Meg Lindsay

Like the O in Hope by Jeanne Julian

A Shape of Sky by Cathy Cain

The Very Rich Hours by Gregory Loselle

Between States of Matter by Sherry Rind

The Kingdom of Birds by Joan Colby

Mary Dyer's Hymn by Stanford Searl

My Mother Never Died Before by Marcia B. Loughran

Mouth Quill by Kaja Weeks

and more . . .

www.ingramcontent.com/pod-product-compliance
Lightning Source LLC
LaVergne TN
LVHW020437080526
838202LV00055B/5238